A SCHOOL FOR
TRINITY

LET THE **REDEEMED** OF THE **LORD** TELL THEIR STORY.

PSALM 107:2

TABLE OF CONTENTS

INTRODUCTION 1

WHICH SCHOOL? 5

THE SAME GOD 15

NOT AGAIN! 33

A NEW YEAR – 2010 42

WILL CAROLINE ROB GOD? 45

A CHANGE OF DIRECTION 51

THE RED SEA 53

A HAVEN IN HARPENDEN 59

ONE LICK! 72

INTRODUCTION

If religious faith is genuine, what does it look like? Is it relational? Does it have a voice? Could it direct or even provide what is needed? Is there even a connection between faith and life on earth? I once had a clear vision while praying. It also seemed to appear on the wall in my hotel room! Let me explain a little further.

It was 2am, and I was awake. My body was relaxed, and I felt no need to continue sleeping. I sat up in bed, listening to the pleasant sound of our daughter's breathing as she lay asleep beside me. The other sound that entertained my ears was the calm waves as they rolled onto the sandy beach outside our hotel window. We were on holiday in St. Lucia. As I was talking to the Lord, an image appeared before me, as if I were watching a giant television screen. My eyes scanned a vast room. It was a library containing a myriad of books.

INTRODUCTION

"Wow, look at that, Lord!" I quietly repeated many times, hoping not to wake my sleeping child.

As I watched, a figure came into sight, which I could only describe as an angel. I could see no door; it simply appeared in the room. It was much larger than a human figure but not human. I saw no wings or facial features, yet it seemed to look in my direction and then turn away. Its feet made no contact with the floor as it hovered slowly across the expansive library. I watched, transfixed. It glided upwards, and on reaching its destination, a long arm unfurled and stretched forward, selecting a small book from one of the library shelves. It then angel floated downward – hugging the book with both arms as though it were a precious object – the size of the book grew to an enormous proportion. It made the angel shrink in comparison. The book was gently placed on a small table, taking its total weight, with the angel and the table hovering off the floor. Slowly, the angel opened the book and began to read aloud. I recognised the text straight away: Hebrews chapter 11. The angel read the whole chapter and, on completion, re-read verse 31, which begins, 'And what more shall I say?' I do not have time ...' and in my spirit, I heard the continuation,

"I do not have time ... but there will be so much more time one day. Much has already been written, and we will read about the active

faith of those commended as the ancients. For it has and it will be recorded."

The angel then read the names of people who had acted upon their faith and what they had achieved, turning page after page. The angel's voice seemed quiet most of the time and became louder when it was a name I recognised. I started crying when I heard my name and the examples of faith given. Then the angel turned to a blank page, but not for long. Print began to appear on the page with someone's name and the act of faith to which they were credited. At that moment, I realised the book was still recording and filling the blank pages with stories of current active faith. I understood that the book would not be complete until the end of time. As the angel closed the book and picked it up, deliberately showing me the front cover, a smile spread across my face, and the vision ended. It had only lasted a minute or two, but I would remain awake for over an hour, reliving and talking to Jesus about the experience.

Now, let's step out of the surreal and into the nitty-gritty of life on earth. The vision was genuine, just as life is real too. I want to take you on a short journey that mirrors the reality of active faith in the 21st century and not just a vision on a wall! I want to share a faith-filled adventure that took me into the unknown. It proved, if I had any doubt, that what I believed, had depth and relevance. It began when

INTRODUCTION

our daughter was two years old. I asked the Lord a question: "Where would *You* like our daughter to go to school?" This question, and I hope the ones above, will be answered as you read *A School for Trinity*.

WHICH SCHOOL?

"But which of them has stood in the council of the Lord to see or to hear his word? Who has listened and heard his word?"

Jeremiah 23:18

Putting our daughter into a private independent school had never crossed our minds. However, Trinity was now two years old. We had to begin thinking about where she would go to school and what preschool she would attend. I started to seek God for direction. I would only decide once I sensed His guidance.

"Where would *You* like us to send her to school?"

I asked that question while sorting out some laundry. I found my mind wandering and becoming anxious about Trinity's future. The inner voice of the Holy Spirit asked me a question,

WHICH SCHOOL?

"What are you doing?

"Well, I'm folding the clothes!" was my not-so-smart reply.

"No, what are you doing?" He asked with greater emphasis.

My thoughts were visible to the Holy Spirit.

"I'm sorry," was my reply, "I began to get anxious!"

"What name have you given to your daughter?"

"Trinity."

"Every time you call her name, whether in frustration or happiness, you declare the Father, the Son, and the Holy Spirit over her. Therefore, you have nothing to worry about. The Trinity covers her life."

"Thank you!"

A year later, the Lord directed me not to put our daughter into preschool. I received no apparent reason; I had to obey and trust His foresight. I thought about her friends starting preschool and other children her age. Was Trinity missing out? Was I doing the right thing? It's natural for the reasoning of our mind to challenge an unfamiliar path. Then, one evening, when I was driving to a friend's house for a time of prayer, I heard in my spirit,

"You're either going to have to trust Me or do what everyone else is doing."

Some scriptures came to my mind.

"Does the LORD delight in burnt offerings and sacrifices as much as in obeying the voice of the LORD? To obey is better than sacrifice."

1Samuel 15:22

So, as the Holy Spirit says: "Today if you hear his voice, do not harden your hearts." **Hebrews 3:7-8**

"Choose for yourselves this day whom you will serve."

Joshua 24:15

"Okay Lord, I'm going to trust your leading," was my heartfelt response.

"I will guide you through this season and determine its length. Do not pursue your own course like a horse charging into battle. Even the stork in the sky knows her appointed seasons, and the dove, the swift, and the thrush observe the time of their migration. But let it not be said of you that you do not know the requirements or the plans of the LORD."

Listen to my instruction and be wise; do not disregard it. Blessed are those who listen to me, watching daily at my doors, waiting at my doorway. **Proverbs 8:33-34**

The months flew by quickly, and Trinity was coming up to her fourth birthday. Over the past year, I had been attending a 'home school' meeting group, but somehow, I knew in my heart that our daughter wouldn't benefit from this long-term. At the time, I had developed and ran two short courses called 'Understanding the Old Testament.' My mind returned to how God desired to lead the Israelites out of Egypt and instil His way of doing things in them. The Israelites were in Egypt for 400 years and had grown accustomed to the Egyptian way of life. Yet the God of Israel wanted his people to do things according to His blueprint. Frequently, the Israelites were told,

"You must not live according to the customs of the nations I will drive out before you." **Leviticus 20:23**

My challenge was to trust the same God who wanted me to do things differently. I had to wait for guidance about the school our daughter attended. Was it easy? Very often, in our fast-paced, instant culture, waiting can be extremely difficult because it means we are not in control. But the Bible encourages us to 'wait on the Lord' and 'be of good courage' while in the waiting. When we race ahead of the Spirit's ushering, we make our own decisions and may miss knowing the will of God.

Three months after Trinity's fourth birthday, a friend's children had been accepted into a Christian School in Kent called Cedars. It was set up by a mother of five children, who felt God was calling her to set up a school for Him and was instructed not to put her children through a state school. I read the booklet about the school's beginning and its ethos. It was a school where they openly loved Jesus. They prayed with the children, and the curriculum was Christian-based. I sat on my friend's settee with mixed emotions: excitement and longing. Tears welled inside me, and I offered an arrow prayer from my heart.

"Oh Lord, You know this is the kind of school I want Trinity to attend."

Then I sensed the Holy Spirit saying,

"Go and visit The King's School in Whitney."

I'd known about this Christian school for over a year, but I dismissed it as being too far, and now the Lord was telling me to go and visit. I rang the school and visited the next day with our daughter. The journey was almost an hour without traffic at ten o'clock in the morning. Surely, that was too long. I looked around the school and talked with the head teacher. Its ethos was very similar to Cedars School, which I had read about. It was set up by a group of parents over twenty years ago who felt God was calling them to set up a Christian school. But was this the right school for Trinity? What was the Lord saying to me? As I spoke to the head teacher in her office,

WHICH SCHOOL?

she mentioned another Christian school I had yet to hear of, stating that it would be a shorter journey. She gave me the phone number, and I left with uncertainty. In the car, I took out the paper from my handbag with the name and phone number of the 'closer' school: Emmanuel Christian School, Littlemore, Oxford. I dialed the number, and no one picked up. I left a message and drove away from The King's School, wondering what direction to take next. Wait, I told myself. Clarity will come.

On arriving home, there was a message from the school. I returned the call and arranged to visit the following day. The drive was thirty minutes and I thought to myself an extra ten minutes in rush hour. My first impression of the school was how small and intimate it was. It didn't feel like an institution but a large family. At that time, the total number of pupils was under 60. Trinity and I looked around the school and chatted with the school secretary. It was set up in 1988 and once again by a group of parents who felt the need for an alternative approach to education. The founding families wanted to put God and a Biblical world-view back into the heart of their children's education. It was a school where the parents were very much involved. Back in the car, I sat with my thoughts. Is God asking me to do this journey every day? This could be the school the Lord wants Trinity to attend. I certainly sensed an inner witness of God's Spirit in my heart, instilling reassurance that this was the school for Trinity.

A SCHOOL FOR TRINITY

At the time, my husband was once again away on business. So, we visited the school two weeks later on his return. This time, the head teacher showed us around. My heart was warmed as she often made comments such as, "The Lord blessed us"; "We are trusting in the Lord"; "We are praying the Lord will..." Her comments put me at ease, and back home, as I read through the school prospectus again, I knew what the Lord was saying. I rang the school, and Trinity was offered a place for September 2008. We had waited on the Lord for two years, and God directed us to the school for Trinity. He told me to trust Him, not to think about it, and He would tell me when to move. The faithfulness of God's character shone through.

The book of Deuteronomy has one of my favourite scriptures: 'We should not live on bread alone but on every word that comes from the mouth of God.' If words proceed from God's mouth, ask yourself, "Am I listening?" Ancient wisdom in Proverbs says God will direct us if we allow Him to lead, especially when it seems illogical? In the book of James, we are reminded not just to hear God's Word but to do it. Put it into practice and be sensitive to the Holy Spirit's leading. I had read about Cedars, visited The King's School, and visited Emmanuel Christian School (ECS), and Trinity was offered a place within seven days. Interestingly, the number seven means completion in God in biblical numerology. When our daughter

WHICH SCHOOL?

Trinity started attending ECS, she told everyone, "I'm going to a school where they love Jesus."

But little did I realise what was ahead. It would open up a new level of trust I was yet to experience.

When God has a purpose for us, the enemy will always try to place doubt in our hearts and minds. The best solution in combating doubt is to know the importance of using God's Word and recognising the promptings of the Holy Spirit. When Jesus was tempted in the wilderness three times, He said, "It is written." What was he referring to? The written Word of God. Each time, He quoted the Old Testament.

A friend said I would use a lot of petrol for the journey. I immediately heard the Holy Spirit reassure me with a scripture I knew, followed by a specific instruction.

"The earth is the LORD's and everything in it. Even the diesel in your car is mine. So, don't be concerned."

Nevertheless, before I started the journey to school, I still had to battle with thoughts: "Is God asking me to drive 20 miles to take our daughter to school each day? That's a 40 mile round trip, Lord. That's not a school run. It's a journey!" Very often, seeds of doubt begin in the mind. The Bible has some advice: we should take every

A SCHOOL FOR TRINITY

thought captive, especially when it is contrary to the Word or will of God in our lives. We must be active in doing this; otherwise, we will give in to the old way of doing things: self-control.

Another obstacle I faced was other people's reactions. Proverbs says, 'fear of man will prove to be a snare.' I had to explain why we had decided to choose a school 20 miles from our home when there were two reasonable schools in the village where we lived. I was quizzed by Christians and those who had no relationship with Jesus. I talked about *my* conviction to send Trinity to a Christian school. Then, one day, while I was praying, the Lord politely reprimanded me: *His* conviction was placed within me. It was not my idea. I had to repent, get off my 'high horse,' and rightfully give God the glory for what He had done and for *His* leading in my heart. Sometimes, it can be easy to bypass what God has done and give ourselves the accolade. It's called pride!

My son, do not despise the Lord's discipline and do not resent his rebuke because the Lord disciplines those he loves, as a father, the son he delights in. **Proverbs 3:11-12**

"Is it recognition you want? Is it approval and praise from others that you seek? Or do you seek to please Me and follow My will? I love you dearly. Pick yourself up when you fall. You are always forgiven. I sent My Son to die for that very reason. I will never withhold My

love from you. You can come to Me again and again when it seems as if you have failed. One day, you will stand perfect in My sight. I want you for Myself. Let Me show you a new level of intimacy on this journey."

Trinity started attending ECS Nursery two and a half days a week in September 2008. On the half day, I tried to find somewhere to pray rather than drive back home. That first morning, I sat in a library conservatory to spend time with our Saviour and thank Him for what he had done. I found a quiet spot. It was freezing in there, so I kept my jacket on. By the end of that morning, my teeth were chattering! The following week, I found a nearby Baptist church to pray in, and the Minister gladly offered me a room. It was much warmer than the library conservatory. As I sat that morning in a state of thanksgiving, I was overwhelmed by the Lord's presence and what He had done in finding Trinity a school. He had given me my heart's desire, and I heard these words within:

"See what I have done. I have answered your prayer as you have trusted and obeyed Me. I have placed your daughter in a school where they love Me, so that you can come into My presence and sit at my feet without being concerned about who is teaching her, or what she is being taught."

It is the Lord's doing, and it's marvelous in our eyes.

Psalm 118:23

THE SAME GOD

From the early days of walking with Jesus, I learned to include Him, and I'm still learning to do so in big and small decisions. He is not just interested in our spiritual life; we are encouraged – even commanded – to cast all our cares on Him because He cares for us. When I was single and looking for accommodation, I went to view a three-bedroom flat. It was clean and spacious, but I thought the rent was too high. I would be living with my sister, who was still at university for another year, so I would be the only one paying the rent. I was working as a full-time teacher and kept thinking, "Can I afford the rent alone?" The cost was £525 per month: it was the early 1990s. I took the matter to the Lord. We had a brief chat that went something like this,

"But Lord, I'm not sure I can afford the rent?"

THE SAME GOD

"Who controls your finances?"

"You do."

"Then move in."

Sometimes, we must trust God when we can't see the way ahead. That's easier said than done, especially as mentioned before; we like to be in charge. But our Heavenly Father always has our best interest at heart and sees beyond the immediate. Within a month of moving into the flat, a friend needed somewhere to live, and she moved into the third empty room, paying a third of the rent. The landlord was the best I have ever had. If there was a problem in the flat, he would rectify it the same day. We lived in the flat for almost seven years and the landlord never raised the rent. Also, before moving in, I asked about the cost of the council tax. He said,

"Oh, don't worry about that, I'll pay it."

There is the confidence that comes, and it only comes when we step out in faith, take a risk, and trust what the Lord is saying. Proverbs urges us to 'Commit our plans to the Lord, and He will cause them to succeed.' Trusting the Lord with all our hearts: with everything that concerns us. Andrew Murray summarises it this way: 'Holding the Word of God in your heart until it has affected every phase of your life.' Understanding from God will always supersede our understanding.

A SCHOOL FOR TRINITY

"For my thoughts are not your thoughts, neither are my ways your ways," declares the LORD. **Isaiah 55:8**

Our daughter had only been at ECS for a month, and my heart needed reassurance (again!) that we had made the right decision. A question had been in my mind: am I odd? It was late, and I got into bed, determined to spend time with the Lord. He answered my question when I wasn't expecting an answer.

"You are not odd. My calling is upon you to do this. This is My purpose for you and Trinity. People thought John the Baptist was odd, yet I called him for a specific purpose. I will bless you in this purpose. You cried to me, "It's not enough, it's not enough! My time with You is not enough!" I heard you. I want to spend more time with you so that you cry out, "Enough, enough!" Because My presence will overwhelm you. My love will have such a deep impact in your heart that you will no longer recognise yourself. Remember when My presence came, and you had to open the shower door? I am coming again in a greater measure. You will begin to experience the height, the width, and the depth of My love like never before. Do not doubt in your heart that I have called you. You are Mine, and you belong to Me. This journey will continue."

"Wow, Lord!"

It is the Lord Christ you are serving. **Colossians 3:24**

It was amazing to hear those words so clearly. I was so excited at what the Lord had shared that I rang my husband, who was away on business and read my journal entry to him. It's a beautiful place to be when you can hear the voice of God's Spirit speaking in your life. I received such peace that night and fell soundly asleep. A few days later, I attended a meeting where the speaker referred to John the Baptist as odd but chosen by God for a specific purpose – an explicit confirmation of what the Lord had already spoken to me.

Oh, shall I tell you about the shower door experience? Of course. I was coming to the end of my first year of teaching, and I was looking forward to a new class. The current one had been a daily challenge on many levels. However, my expectation was short-lived as the headteacher asked me to continue teaching the class for another year. I felt daunted by her request and said I would think about it and let her know the following morning. Later that evening, I shared my heart with the Lord. What?! I sensed the Holy Spirit gently saying that I should take the same class another year. A directive I was not pleased about. So, I spent some time explaining (in great detail) why I couldn't teach again, giving all my justifications.

"Lord, they are *so* naughty and incredibly demanding. I have even found that I can shout! No, Lord, I'm not going to do that. I can't face this class for another year. It's too stressful. Last week I even hid and cried in my classroom cupboard at the end of the day!"

Once again in my life, I could sense the struggle of, "Not my will but Yours be done." That evening, standing in the shower cubicle, I repositioned my heart and said yes to the Lord. Well, His presence filled the small shower unit and as I opened the shower door I exclaimed,

"Your presence and I cannot fit in this small shower cubicle together!" I giggled and continued, "Some of *You* needs to come out!"

That second year with the class was not as difficult as I thought it would be. They already knew me and my expectations. It also gave me the experience and strategies to teach other challenging classes later in my teaching career.

Okay, back to *A School for Trinity*. Then, this happened: four weeks after our daughter had started ECS, her father was made redundant. By the end of the year 2008, he was still out of work. In January, Trinity began full-time in Reception class, and a term of school fees loomed ahead of us. One evening, George and I discussed taking our daughter out of school for a term, until he found work. My burdensome heart slowly sank as I cleared away the dishes, and inwardly I poured out my distress.

"Lord, how can this be? I've waited for You to show me where Trinity should attend school and now, we can't pay the fees. She's only just started."

I read the scripture on our window sill and reasoned with myself.

"Caroline, do you believe that scripture? Would God show you somewhere, give you direction and then not provide for what is needed?"

Trying to convince myself didn't work!

"Oh Lord, it's a lot of money. How are we going to pay for it? What are we going to do?"

I read the scripture on the window sill again.

"Do not be anxious about anything, but in everything, by prayer and petition, with thanksgiving, present your requests to God. And the peace of God, which transcends all understanding, will guard your hearts and minds through Christ." **Philippians 4:6-7**

"Do you believe My Word? What have you just read? How long has that scripture sat on your window sill? Are they just empty words to you?"

Could I answer all those questions positively? My conversation with the Lord continued as I washed the dishes, and a sense of peace began to creep in.

"Okay, Lord. Trinity going to ECS was not my idea. It was Yours. I know You directed me, so I will not fret and worry, even though that's what I feel like doing. *You* even told me that *Your* conviction was placed within me to send Trinity to ECS. Therefore, I have no choice but to trust You to provide the finances somehow."

"I see everything that's taking place in your heart and mind. Please don't allow it to control you. Be guided by My Word. Be transformed by the renewing of your mind. Continue to swear in a truthful, just and righteous way, 'As surely as the LORD lives,' and you will see My blessings come. Those who fear Me, small and great, will be blessed."

My heart felt steadfast and settled. I had nowhere else to turn. Four days later, God's Spirit spoke to someone,

"Caroline, I don't want you to worry about Trinity's school fees for next term. God has told me to pay it."

I couldn't believe what I heard, so I asked my friend to repeat her offer! I informed her of the possible cost: £1,300.

"That's okay," was her cheerful response, "God has told me to pay it. You'll have the cheque by the end of the week."

THE SAME GOD

Oh my goodness me! Tears of thankfulness welled up in my eyes. Wow, how quick was that! Somehow, somewhere inside of me, I knew He would. I just didn't expect it to happen in four days!"

"When my children are obedient, the Kingdom of Heaven works as it should on earth."

"Do you not know? Have you not heard? The LORD is the everlasting God, the Creator of the ends of the earth. He will not grow tired or weary, and his understanding no one can fathom."

Isaiah 40:28

Back at school in January 2009, I received the invoice for the school fees. Trinity's nursery grant covered £500, and my obedient friend paid the £800. A few days later, at church, the speaker talked about God planting seeds in our lives. He used Smarties to represent seeds, as a queue of children lined up waiting for a "Smartie seed" to be placed in their hand. Trinity was last in the queue. She held her hand out to receive her Smartie, and the speaker said,

"But sometimes God does not want to plant a single seed."

A very disappointed Trinity began walking away, thinking there was no "Smartie seed" left for her, until the speaker called,

"No! Come back, come back, Trinity!"

He told Trinity to cup both her hands together, and he poured the rest of the Smarties into her hands, saying,

"Sometimes, God wants to plant lots of seeds in our lives!"

That evening, as I prayed before going to bed, I heard,

"Cup your hands like your daughter did today. I want to fill them with spiritual smarties, blessings from Heaven. This is a Word from Me to you for the year ahead."

I was beaming from ear to ear.

****

It was a dark, wet Monday morning in March. The rain was beating ferociously on the windscreen as I drove along the A40 towards Littlemore in Oxford. I was weary and feeling unwell. A thought came into my mind: "Did God really say that Trinity should go to ECS and that I should do this journey daily?" I entertained this thought for the rest of the morning, struggling with a Spirit-led directive and my emotions. "Oh, hello doubt. Come inside and sit down. Would you like a cup of tea? I've just baked a cake. Would you like a slice? Tell me, what's been happening in your life? The weather is changing, so why don't you stay for lunch? I have enough for the two of us. Let's go for a walk this afternoon. My, it's getting late, why don't you stay the night in the spare room? This journey is wearing you out." All day, somewhere in the back of my mind, I doubted and entertained the thought, "Did God say...?" Isn't that what the serpent said to Eve in the Garden of Eden?

"Did God say, 'You must not eat from any tree in the garden?'"

Genesis 3:1

That evening, just before our meal, Trinity looked at me and said,

"Mummy, when Jesus died, the curtain ripped in half, ripped!"

How interesting that Trinity had made such a comment. At school that day, she had been taught about the Tabernacle. I asked her what she meant, and she replied,

"The Tabernacle was a place where people like Joseph, Moses, and the Priests went to pray. When Jesus died on the cross, the curtain in the Tabernacle ripped in two, and anybody who loves Jesus can go into the Tabernacle and pray."

I sat there – amazed – as I listened to our four-year-old daughter.

"That is the answer to the question from this morning, 'Did God say?"

Our daughter had given me the reassurance I needed, and I was reminded of a scripture.

From the lips of children and infants, you have ordained praise.

Psalm 8:2

Emotions can be overwhelmingly real against the backdrop of God's Word in our lives. But deep down, I knew I was doing what God had asked: driving 20 miles to take our daughter to a "school where they loved Jesus."

The following morning, as I drove to school, we both sang along to a worship song declaring that Jesus was our everything. I stopped to put diesel in the car, and as I stood in the queue to pay, I sensed a real closeness from the Lord. I could only describe it as a tangible, heart-warming "force." The sensation moved with me to the front of the queue. It was surreal but, at the same time, thrilling! I looked at the woman over the counter. She was in the natural, seen world. In my spirit, I asked,

"What was that, Lord?"

"My presence with you."

As I returned to the car, His presence moved with me: tactile and embracing. I drove off, and Trinity insisted I repeatedly play the same worship song.

'God in my living, there in my breathing
God in my waking, God in my sleeping
God in my resting, there in my working
God in my thinking, God in my speaking

Be my everything, be my everything
Be my everything, be my everything

God in my hoping, there in my dreaming
God in my watching, God in my waiting
God in my laughing, there in my weeping
God in my hurting, God in my healing

Be my everything, be my everything
Be my everything, be my everything

Christ in me, Christ in me
Christ in me, the hope of glory
You are everything' [1]

The Easter holiday of 2009 had come to an end, and my husband had been out of work for six months. We knew Trinity was still entitled to a nursery grant and we also applied for a school bursary.

---

[1] Be my Everything by Tim Hughes

I knew her nursery grant could be a bit more than the previous term. If we were unsuccessful with the bursary application, the cost of the school fees would be approximately £700. Before the Easter holiday, one of the school's governors rung me concerning our bursary application. By the end of the phone call my faith was almost zero that we would receive the financial assistance we needed. Feeling very anxious I prayed and felt reassured that God would somehow make a way. He did it before, so why wouldn't He do it again? My reasoning screamed that such trust was illogical, but a scripture again counter-acted it.

"For my thoughts are not your thoughts, neither are your ways my ways," declares the LORD. "As the heavens are higher than the earth, so are my ways higher than your ways and my thoughts than your thoughts." **Isaiah 55:8-9**

Later that day, I read these words from a devotional book I had been using since the beginning of the year. 'I am with you to guide you and help you. Unseen forces are controlling your destiny. Your petty fears are groundless. What if a man walking through a glorious glade fretted because there lay a river ahead, and he might not be able to cross it when that river was spanned by a bridge all the time? And what if that man had a friend who knew the way – had planned it – and assured him that at no part of the journey would any

THE SAME GOD

unforeseen contingency arise and that all was well? So leave your foolish fears. Follow Me, Your Guide, and refuse to consider tomorrow's problems. My message to you is, trust and wait.'[2]

Not too long after, a friend gave me a list of scriptures, and there was one in particular that the Holy Spirit spoke to me about: the widow's oil. It is found in the book of 2 Kings, chapter 4. It tells the story of a woman whose husband had died. He belonged to the company of prophets, and she was now in dire poverty. She sought the advice of a prophet called Elisha.

"Your servant, my husband is dead, and you know that he revered the LORD. But now the creditor is coming to enslave my two boys."

"How can I help you? Tell me, what do you have in your house?" Elisha asked.

"Your servant has nothing there at all," she said, "except a little oil."

Elisha responded,

"Go round and ask all your neighbours for empty jars. Don't ask for just a few. Then go inside and shut the door behind you and your sons. Pour oil into all the jars, and as each is filled, put it to one side."

---

[2] God Calling edited by A.J. Russell

She left him and shut the door behind her and her sons. They brought the jars to her, and she kept pouring. When all the jars were full, she said to her son,

"Bring me another one." But he replied,

"There is not a jar left."

Then, the oil stopped flowing. She told the man of God, and he said, "Go, sell the oil, and pay your debts. You and your sons can live on what is left." **2 Kings 4:1-7**

"I am the same God yesterday, today and forever. I do not change. As I multiplied the widow's oil, I will multiply the little that you have."

"But Lord, I don't even have a little!" I said with a giggle, and the Lord replied,

"You have worked for two hours doing supply cover at ECS, although I asked you not to work. I am going to multiply that money."

"Sorry, Lord."

"Just trust Me."

A couple of days later, I went to an evening prayer meeting, and the only scripture read was the widow's oil.

The traffic was heavy on the way to school. Then, we were hardly moving. We would be late again, and I was helping in the classroom that morning. A few cars whizzed past me in the bus lane. I joined them only to be met by the arm of the law at the end. The police officer was joyful and polite, as he handed me a fine of £30. Oh dear, I would have to use the ECS supply money to cover the cost of the fine. I was paid £22. It didn't cover the cost of the fine. The Lord was left with £8 to multiply!

"Oh, Caroline," I was talking to myself, "you're not supposed to make things worse!"

But God had given me His Word and the comfort of a scripture despite me breaking the law! I was reminded of Abraham when God told him his wife Sarah would give birth to a son when she was old: 90 years. Although Abraham believed in God's Word, he still messed up. Now, if you think driving in the bus lane was terrible, listen to what Abraham did: he slept with his maidservant, and she became pregnant! God's Word will surely come to pass when we walk in faith and obedience. Even when we mess up! The God of the Bible has a redemptive Spirit, redeeming what we can't. A few weeks later, on returning home from school, I heard the following as I bent down to pick up the post,

"There's something there for you."

I had recently found out that I was possibly paying too much tax. Now, all the envelopes were white. I reasoned that mail from the Inland Revenue usually came in brown envelopes. So, I dismissed what I had heard and became busy in the kitchen. Eventually, an hour or so later, I opened the post. I took out a letter from a white envelope. It was from the Inland Revenue stating that I had paid too much tax. I unfolded the flap at the bottom to read the amount: £2,810.35! It was a jaw-dropper I hadn't expected! The £8 had been multiplied by 351! That's called Bible mathematics and another very big Smartie!

"My word will not return to me empty, but will it accomplish what I desire and achieve the purpose for which I send it out."

Isaiah 55:11

In his book, *The Grand Weaver,* Ravi Zacharias points out that God often reinforces our faith after we trust him, not before. It means we must take risks in the Lord and trust what He is saying to us. Amazingly, Abraham saw God's provision when he obediently offered his son Isaac as a sacrifice. He trusted in God's Sovereignty, and when his son asked where the sacrifice was, Abraham answered,

"The Lord will provide."

We took a risk by leaving our daughter at ECS because God said, and I had arrived at a place where I could certainly say,

"He is and always will be the definition of one of His names: Jehovah Jireh – The Lord Will Provide."

NOT AGAIN!

It was September 2009, and Trinity was returning to school after the summer break with my husband still out of work. Here we go again!

"Caroline," talking to myself another time, "this is another opportunity for you to prove God again!"

Now, am I thinking that based on faith, weariness, or sheer disbelief, we were still in the same position? The day before, at church, I was asked to teach Sunday school at short notice. We were talking about Bible characters and had illustrated cards. A boy called Joseph picked up Martha's character and explained that she was Mary's sister and had lots of empty containers God filled with oil so it wouldn't run out. The characters didn't link with the story, but I certainly knew where the story had come from. The following day, as I was driving home from school listening to a worship CD and thinking about the Lord, I heard,

"Don't forget my Word spoke to you yesterday."

"What Word, Lord? I wasn't in church to hear the message; I was teaching in Sunday school."

"My Word was given to you through the child Joseph."

Instantly, I knew what Word the Lord meant: the widow's oil. The same Word He had told me to trust in some months ago.

"You can still use it. It hasn't expired. There is no 'use-by date' on it. It can be used over and over again. My Word is settled."

"Thank you, the Lord."

How quickly we can sometimes forget God's Word when the reality of life comes knocking.

A week later, at home time, I was given an envelope containing the school fees. That day there was also a short school prayer meeting at the end of the day, as it had been a week of prayer. I decided to open the envelope after the meeting. Whatever the amount was, I wanted my mind to be clear to pray.

An hour later, I sat in the car with the envelope on my lap. Should I open it now or wait until I get home? Trinity was munching through a bag of crisp in the back of the car, and I opened the envelope. My heart sank, like a lead weight as I looked at the amount for the autumn term: £848. Within seconds, my emotional state deteriorated, and my silent cry spoke to the Lord,

"Lord, I'm not showing this to George. This invoice is for You. How on earth are we going to pay this Lord? George has been out of work for nearly eleven months and You have instructed me not to return to work. We don't have the money to pay for this."

On arriving home, my anxiety intensified. It seemed as if nothing could dampen the sense of foreboding creeping through me. Even Trinity sensed that something was wrong.

"Mummy, are you sad?" I looked at her and said,

"No lovely. I'm just thinking about something."

Was I sad? No, I felt overwhelmed by the figure of 848. Trinity went into the conservatory to play. I retreated into the kitchen to pray and offload on the Lord.

"Lord, how are we going to pay this? If I must remove Trinity from Emmanuel Christian School, I'm not putting her into a state school because I know Your Spirit has led me. I'll have to home-school her."

My head was spinning as I thought about the uncertainty of the future ahead. I looked at Trinity dancing in the conservatory. Her arms were lifted above her head, and she was singing one of her made-up songs to Jesus.

"Jesus, Jesus, I love you," she sang repeatedly as she jumped on her small trampoline. I turned away, tears in my eyes, and prayed.

"That's why she can't leave ECS. She's singing to You, Lord, she's singing to You."

Later that evening, I took a scripture from the small promise box that sat on on our kitchen table. This was the prayer:

'Heavenly Father, remind me that You are always ready to help us through life, no matter how difficult things may seem.'

There was also a scripture verse to go with it. I picked up my Bible and read the whole chapter.

I look up to the mountains – does my help come from there? My help comes from the LORD, who made the heavens and the earth! He will not let you stumble and fall; the one who watches over you will not sleep. Indeed, he who watches over Israel never tires and never sleeps. The LORD himself watches over you! The LORD stands beside you as your protective shade. The sun and the moon will not hurt you by day or night. The LORD keeps you from all evil and preserves your life. The LORD keeps watch over you as you come and go, both now and forever. **Psalm 121**

Peace came, and once again, momentarily, my emotions settled. However, the next few days still involved a battle to trust the authority of God's Word. I wanted everyone to know our predicament. Yet the Holy Spirit urged me to tell no one.

"So do not fear, for I am with you; do not be dismayed, for I am your God. I will strengthen and help you; I will uphold you with my righteous right hand." **Isaiah 41:10**

"We don't know what to do, but our eyes are upon you."
2 Chronicles 20:12

In my thoughts, the enemy would say, "Where is your God now?" Spiritually, I was up and down. One moment, I would feel victorious. At other times, I thought I was the laughing stock of those who questioned or doubted my actions. On other occasions, my mind would taunt me with, "How are the school fees going to be paid now?" Yet in the early hours of one morning, while in the bathroom, I heard my spirit declaring a familiar psalm – often read at funerals – which brought much-needed comfort.

The LORD is my shepherd. I shall not want. He makes me lie down in green pastures; he leads me beside the quiet waters; he restores my soul. He leads me in the paths of righteousness, for his name's sake. Even though I walk through the valley of the shadow of death, I will fear no evil, for you are with me; your rod and your staff comfort me. You prepare a table before me in the presence of my enemies. You anoint my head with oil; my cup overflows. Surely, goodness and mercy will follow me all the days of my life, and I will dwell in the house of the LORD forever.

Psalm 23

"Lord, how?"

"Only by faith."

"Where is it?"

"Inside of you."

Promptly, I discovered it! Faith. It was in me at that very point in time. I found it. My emotions were stilled, and the turmoil ceased. In the natural, things seemed irrational. Yet, I knew the reality of who was leading me. I could trust in the gift of faith within me, and I wanted to shout aloud, "Why didn't someone tell me this before?" But I didn't because it was 5am!

I had received the school invoice on Tuesday. It was now Friday. I had to show it to my husband, George. My fear was unfounded.

Despite the £848, he still desired our daughter to remain at ECS, and he quoted one of the earliest scriptures I memorised when I began to read the Bible consistently. We were of one mind.

"And we know that in all things God works for the good of those who love him, who have been called according to his purpose."

Romans 8:28

My head was clear, and God had raised a standard over my fears. His Word to me was sure. Don't trust your feelings. Don't listen to the enemy and dance with doubt. Wait and see what God will do.

"Who *(or what)* shall separate us from the love of Christ? Shall trouble or hardship ... *(or school fees?)* No, in all these things, we are more than conquerors through him who loved us."

Romans 8:35, 37

"Heaven and earth will pass away, but My word will stand forever."

Matthew 24:35

I sent an email regarding the fees. The total amount of credit from the previous term, and expenses for me cleaning the school had not been accounted for. Two days later, I received a reply with an amended amount of £504. I thanked the Lord for the reduced amount, trusting that somehow we would be able to pay the lower figure. Two weeks later, I walked into the school office with £10 in my hand. The £10 was part of £45 that a friend slipped into my jacket pocket. I had to pay £5 for a school trip and asked the secretary if she had received the updated invoice from the treasurer. She informed me that she had, and the total school fees for the term was £4.

"£4," I repeated, a little perplexed.

"What about the rest of it, £500?"

"It's been paid."

"What do you mean it's been paid?"

"Someone has paid the £500 for you, and I'm not obliged to say who."

Oh my goodness! I didn't know whether to laugh, cry, scream, or jump up and down! All I could say was "Praise God!" repeatedly. I paid for the school trip, £5. I paid the school fees of £4 and put the £1 in the school kitty! I rang my husband to tell him the fantastic news and rejoiced all the way home. God had kept His Word. A friend recently said that God would send us pennies from heaven. We certainly received some that day straight from Heaven's bank!

"For I know the plans I have for you," declares the LORD, "plans to prosper you and not to harm you, plans to give you hope and a future. Then you will call upon me and come and pray to me, and I will listen to you." **Jeremiah 29:11-12**

"I move at a different pace to you. I move in peace, which passes human understanding. That peace was there for you when you received the invoice for the school fees. You could have dwelt in that peace that passes understanding, but you gave in to what the enemy was saying to your emotions. You trusted Me to find a school for Trinity. The only two real obstacles were the enemy and yourself. Obstacles are nothing to Me. I blow them out of the way as you trust in the authority of My Word. All you had to do was trust My Word, and then you would have had peace which passes all understanding."

A NEW YEAR — 2010

Lord, I will remember what you have done and choose to wait for your counsel.

Psalm 106:13

It was the start of a new year. The Holy Spirit had already reminded me of what the Lord did in 2009. I reread the tales in my journal. What an adventure it had been! 2010 was a few days old. George was still out of work, and we would have to trust again in the same God. Yes, here we go again!

"You gave your good Spirit to instruct them. You did not withhold your manna from their mouths and gave them water for their thirst. For forty years, you sustained them in the desert; they lacked nothing, their clothes did not wear out, nor did their feet become swollen."

Nehemiah 9:20-21

I knew the same Spirit that led and instructed Israel was there for our benefit. The same God would sustain the Harrigan-Brown family in the 21st century as He did in the days of old for Israel. God would take care of our tomorrows. He will provide for us as He provided for Israel and as He provided for us in 2009. We serve a God who never changes.

"Jesus Christ, the same yesterday, today, and forever."

Hebrews 13:8

Our insistence on discerning what's ahead is natural, but it can be a real hindrance to active faith. That is why God constantly encourages us to trust Him in the dark.

"Who among you fears the LORD and obeys the word of his servant? If you are walking in darkness, without a ray of light, trust in the LORD and rely on your God."

Isaiah 50:10

'True faith means resting in who God is. He has charged Himself with full responsibility for our eternal happiness, and He stands ready to take over the management of our lives. He is wise and good. Trust God with what's ahead.' How wonderful that the Lord speaks to us and the reality of who He is, even in this age of technological advancement. We don't know it all!

Trinity returned to school on Tuesday, January 5th. That afternoon, I received a phone call from a friend saying that the Lord had woken her up at 4am to pray for me. She also informed me that they would be paying Trinity's school fees for the term.

"Wow, Lord, that was quick!"

WILL CAROLINE ROB GOD?

Depending on your belief, the area of tithing may be a part of your life or something done in the Old Testament. Many authors have addressed this subject of tithing, which is not the aim here. I will once again highlight the faithfulness of who God is, His Word being reliable and active faith. Whatever you believe, I hope this next section encourages you to trust the Word of the LORD in your life.

During my student days at university, I was taught about tithing early in my Christian walk. Back then, I started to tithe my student grant and continued the practice, believing it to be one of many biblical principles for Christian living.

"Will a man rob God? Yet you have robbed Me! But you say, 'In what way have we robbed you?' In tithes and offerings. You are cursed with a curse, for you have robbed Me, even this nation. Bring all the tithes into the storehouse, that there may be food in My house, and try Me now in this," says the LORD of hosts, "If I will not open for you the windows of heaven and pour out for you such blessing that there will not be room enough to receive it."

Malachi 3:8-10

I handed my tithe to a friend to put in the church offering, since I knew I wouldn't be attending church the following Sunday. By the end of the week, I knew my finances would be nil. I had determined in my heart that I wouldn't ask George for any money but instead trust the Lord to provide me with whatever I needed. However, my friend didn't make it to church that Sunday, and later on in the week, she handed me back the envelope that contained my tithe of £30. So, there in my hand, I had some money. Now, what should I do? Some would say that God gave me back the money as a blessing. However, the thought that kept going around in my mind was,

"Will Caroline rob God?"

Well, at the beginning of the week, I said I would trust God, and that's what I had to do. No, this money doesn't belong to me, and on Sunday, my tithe went in the offering container along with the only money I had left in my purse at the end of the week: a pound coin. I decided, many years ago, that I would not discuss with the Lord how much I should put in the offering plate. I would simply put the highest monetary value – a penny or a pound, £5 or £50 – that was in my purse. That Sunday morning at church, Trinity was flicking through my Bible and found an unopened birthday invitation a friend had given me the previous day. She opened it and within the card pulled out a £20 note! After church, I used it to put diesel in the car.

"Thank you, Lord, I can drive to school in the morning!"

By Tuesday, my logic concluded I would have to keep Trinity at home by the end of the week as the fuel in my car could run out. Oh ye of little faith! On Wednesday, someone slipped £10 in my hand. The same day, a friend asked if I could drop her to the supermarket. As I walked in with her, she pulled out a large shopping trolley and said, "That's yours, fill it!" When we got home that evening, a Tesco voucher for £5.50 was on the doorstep. I've never been so grateful for a Tesco voucher!

A few days later, a friend I had been praying with gave me this Word from the Lord.

"Keep trusting Me for finances. Cast your worries at My feet in an instant, especially at times when you feel overwhelmed. When a thought of lack comes to you, rejoice and be thankful that I will provide. Walk with an attitude of faith and confidence. Faith,

confidence, and peace will be your strength. God is your provider in everything. You will remain in My presence when you learn to trust in Me completely."

She then gave me the following scripture:

Isaac planted crops in that land and, the same year, reaped a hundredfold because the Lord blessed him. **Genesis 26:12**

In my heart, I believed the scripture but in my mind, I thought, "Great Lord, I'm sure that scripture is for the distant future, but could you send us a few more pennies, please? I have used the Tesco voucher." The following day, when returning from school, I picked up the post, and an envelope was addressed 'To George and Caroline' containing £80. I was lost for words.

"Wow, Lord! Thank you so much!"

The next morning day, just before leaving for school, I attempted to powder my nose with the almost non-existent amount of powder that was left.

"I think the Lord will have to send me another blessing so I can buy a new compact powder. This one is finished," I said to Trinity.

"Mum, you just got a blessing yesterday. You mustn't be greedy! You have to wait a few days before getting another blessing!"

A SCHOOL FOR TRINITY

I laughed out loud and said, "Okay, Trinity."

A few days later as we got ready for church, Trinity complained of a tummy ache, and I didn't feel too great either. We still went and once again, my hand received an envelope. At home, I gave Trinity the envelope to open, and she announced holding each note in the air,

"£20, £10, £10, £10."

There was the fulfilment of Trinity's words. We had waited a few days and received another blessing. I remembered a phrase written in my journal that my Pastor at the time would often quote,

"Real people, real lives, real God."[3]

I learned an old hymn some years ago, and one line reads, 'Showers of blessing, showers of blessings we need, dear Lord.' In a matter of days the following transpired. It was pouring with rain outside: torrential, with a howling wind. I was in the lounge relaxing before leaving at 2:15 pm to go and pick up Trinity from school. I heard the letterbox flap and thought of the poor person posting flyers in the wet deluge. I continued to relax for another twenty minutes before heading to the front door. It wasn't a flyer, but an envelope

---

[3] Quote from Pastor Geoff Blease of the church (Chiltern Christian fellowship) I attended in Princes Risborough

addressed to me and my husband with the words 'An Anonymous Gift.' I opened the envelope to find a cheque for £1000! It took my breath away, and I burst into tears. I'm even crying now while typing this! What could I do but give thanks to such a faithful God?

"Wow, Lord!"

I told Trinity that the Lord had sent us another blessing, enough for me to buy a new powder.

"Is there enough to buy me a new toy?" Trinity asked.

"Yes, my lovely, there's enough!"

I remembered the scripture given to me from Genesis 26:12 and about reaping a hundredfold. We had received more than a hundredfold. That evening, we prayed together as a family, thanking the Lord for His unique provision that week. Our prayer time concluded with Trinity's prayer.

"Lord Jesus, please send us more money so we are not poor. Anyway, we're not because we know You in our lives, and You make us rich! Amen."

A CHANGE OF DIRECTION

As I opened our front door, I heard,

"I'm about to take Trinity out of Emmanuel Christian School, but I don't want you to be concerned."

I stood still in the way, feeling concerned, and Trinity squeezed past me.

"Okay, Lord. I think I just heard you say something to me. I'm going into the kitchen to cook. We'll talk later," I said, pondering what I had just heard.

A few days prior, I rang an independent Christian school in Harpenden out of curiosity and asked them to send me a prospectus. A day after I heard the above Words from the Lord, my

A CHANGE OF DIRECTION

husband informed me out of sheer interest, he had sent an email to the King's School in Harpenden asking for a prospectus. In complete amazement, I exclaimed I had done the same thing earlier in the week and shared what the Lord had said to me the day before when I walked through the front door. We prayed, and the following morning – Saturday – we talked about driving over to Harpenden to see where the school was and look around the area. However, we were reluctant to take Trinity, so we decided against the idea. Within half an hour, a friend rang us to ask if he could take Trinity out for the day with their daughter.

It had been almost two years of driving over to Littlemore in Oxford. During that time, selling our home was only an option once George had a secure job. On several occasions when I attempted to look for possible properties in the Oxford area, the Holy Spirit would say,

"You don't need to do that."

Once Trinity had been picked up, we drove over to discover Harpenden. Two days later, after being out of work for some time, George was offered a job in a city adjacent to Harpenden: St. Albans. To my surprise, we were on the move, and it wasn't Oxford.

THE RED SEA

It was four weeks to the end of the summer holiday. For the last twenty-four hours, I felt anxious about driving Trinity to school in Harpenden, Hertfordshire from our home in Princes Risborough, Buckinghamshire. The offer on our house had fallen through, and in addition, the house we had made an offer on was no longer in our grasp. That night, the Holy Spirit reminded me of a scripture I had been singing that day.

"May the God of hope fill you with all joy and peace, as you trust in Him, so that you may overflow with hope by the power of the Holy Spirit." **Romans 15:13**

A devotional reading gave me some further encouragement:

THE RED SEA

'Yes! Remember that I am always leading you to light out of the darkness. Out of unrest to rest. Out of disorder to order. Out of faults and failures to perfection. So trust Me wholly. Fear nothing. Hope ever. Look up to Me, and I will be your sure aid. My Father and I are One. So He who made the ordered; beautiful world out of chaos; set the stars in their courses; and made each plant know its season; can He not bring out of your little chaos, peace and order? And He and I are One, and you are Mine. Your affairs are Mine. It is My divine task to order My affairs – therefore yours will be ordered by Me.'[4]

It was five days to the start of a new school year – 2010 – and a new school. I was mentally preparing my mind to do the journey. Harpenden was further than Littlemore. An extra ten miles further from Princes Risborough. That evening, Trinity chose a scripture from the little scripture box and handed it to me.

"As I was with Moses, I will be with you." **Joshua 3:7**

The following morning, as I prayed, I was reminded of a book I had just finished reading to ask the Holy Spirit what His divine plan was. A friend came to my mind. I sensed that I should contact her because she would be open for us to stay at her home during the week. This meant the journey time and miles would be considerably

---

[4] God Calling edited by A.J. Russell

reduced. I hadn't had much contact with her over the last year and spent some hours checking with the Lord if this was His leading. I recalled the scripture: "Faith without works is dead." My rational was she could only say "No," and there was no harm in asking. I phoned her later that evening, and her response was,

"I don't need to think about it or pray about it, the answer is yes."

"Wow, Lord!

She informed me that she had been fostering for the last year and only that morning received an email stating that her foster child would not be returning since she had turned 18. The spare room in her home would be vacant immediately. The journey to school would be a twenty-minute drive rather than an hour. To quote a friend,

"God's timing is impeccable!"

"The LORD has sent me....and it was not my idea."
Numbers 16:25

It was a new season for us all. My husband was settling into his new job. Trinity was making new friends at her new school, and I began asking the Lord for direction regarding my life. During my time in Oxford, through God's leading, I was shown three different places where I could go and spend time with Jesus.[5] Harpenden was new territory. My days had no structure. I had to find new places to pray, make new friends, and seek to know why the Lord had moved us to a new county. I found two churches in the town whose doors were always open. On other days, I would meet George for lunch, and have the option of going to the cathedral in St. Albans or a Baptist church to pray. I thought about returning to work or finding a job that would fit around school and term time.

"Lord, I have no plans of my own and don't know which way to turn. I need Your plans. God gave You a plan and made a way for humanity to be saved. Cause me to know the plan in Your heart for me. Open my ears to hear. Cause me to hear Your majestic voice. Cause me to rise and listen to You so I hear what You have to say."

Later that day, I read an email from a friend about the importance of following God's plan, and my devotional reading stated, 'Many of us never get around to fulfilling God's purpose for our lives.' I prayed that I would not fall into that category and that God's plan would be so clear that I wouldn't miss it. As the weeks and months passed, I would frequently hear,

---

[5]The International Centre of Newman friends: Littlemore; Bible Society; All Saints Sisters of the Poor: Headington.

"In time, I will show you your job description."

"Woe to those who go to great depths to hide their plans from the Lord." **Isaiah 29:15**

Over the next few months, I would write many journal entries while waiting for direction and guidance from the Holy Spirit. Let me share just a few:

"Remember My Word to you that this is a season in which I have called you to listen, come into My presence, and pray. This period of time will lay a foundation in your life, and it will bear fruit. People will not understand why you are doing this. They do not need to know, for I have spoken to you. My Word in their life will be different. Your desire is to hear from Me. This must be done in a timely manner. The quality of your relationship with Me will change. You have already begun to see that."

"This will be a lonely journey. Many choose to avoid taking this path. But you have chosen well. My Voice is indeed the Supreme Voice. I will open your ears to hear Me more clearly and cause you to understand My Spirit. Take your eyes off the flesh; it counts for nothing, for no flesh shall glory in My presence. I will teach you how to pray. My definition and My job description of the watchman in his tower. I will show you what is to come. Do not be quick to leave. In

the waiting, you will learn. You are on My journey. Look at the journey My Son took to Calvary for the whole of humanity, and you will realise how easy your journey is. My Son's passion to do My will led Him to the cross."

"You have consecrated your time to Me; your life to Me; and all I would have you to be. Therefore, I will show you everything I want you to be and do in time. There is still so much I need to strip away so you can accept my job description. I will show you who you are to be and how you are to walk."

"My sheep hear my voice and recognise it."   **John 10:27**

A HAVEN IN HARPENDEN

It was a cold, wet February morning as Trinity and I got into the car to journey to school. After five months, we could no longer stay at our friend's home, which meant a reduction in miles, time, and fuel. In my mind, God had not provided a solution. The Red Sea was still before me: the long drive to school. God's timing did not reflect my time scale. I was frustrated and disappointed as I drove across the three counties: Buckinghamshire, Bedfordshire, and Hertfordshire. I couldn't understand why the Lord had not given me another solution.

"Do not be dismayed. Fear not, for I am with you."

"Lord, how long will I have to do this journey?"

I had been sitting alone for about an hour before the Lord in the large Baptist church in St. Albans. The stress I felt brought me to tears.

"Lord, I've got myself into such a state about driving back and forth from school. What have you got to say to me?"

"Can you remember which robe you chose?"

Ah, the robe. I had chosen the filthy one. The previous Sunday at church, a friend gave me the following, written in a card.

'As I was praying for you, God gave me a picture of Jesus hanging on the cross, and it was the garment He was wearing that God caused me to focus on. It looked like a dirty sackcloth: a robe of suffering. But it was one He chose willingly to wear, and because He wore it in complete obedience, as a result, He had victory over death, sin, and Hades.

I felt God say that He has an exceptional place for you that few people attain. It is a very high place of intimacy and calling that is only reached by wearing that filthy rag of His suffering, where all your flesh is dead, and your whole life is focused not on your needs but on the needs of those around you.

There is a price to carry Jesus' glory and to reach that incredible place of intimacy where your heart beats as His heart beats. You will reach it, but not by your effort. He has called you whatever the price. Are you willing to pay for it?

I saw you in the front line – breaking through and making a way for thousands to follow you. But you need to keep your eyes on Him and not on the storm. It will be a lonely place but a place of immense honour and privilege. Immense obedience and total love to everyone, total humility – His hands, voice, feet, and heart.

Are you willing to pay the price? Two robes are available for you – one filthy rag and one royal robe. Jesus chose the filthy rag, and because He did, He also received the one of royalty and majesty. The choice is yours, and I know you will choose wisely.'

"Upon My advice, you chose the robe of suffering. Do you want to change your mind? Are you weary already? On this path, you will learn not to live the rest of your earthly life for evil human desires but rather for the will of God. The Red Sea you think you have come to is not there. The Red Sea is your fear. My Word says not to give way to fear. Cast all your anxiety on Me because I care for you. And the God of all grace, who has called you to His eternal glory in Christ, after you have suffered a while, will restore you and make you strong, firm, and steadfast. This momentary affliction will soon pass.

See how faith rises within you when you talk to others about My agenda in your life. Take your eyes off the school journey, for you can do everything through Me as I strengthen you. These things come so that your faith – of much greater worth than gold, which perishes even though refined by fire – may be proved genuine and result in praise, glory, and honour when I am revealed. Do you think this cross is too heavy to bear? It's only heavy in your strength. Submit it to me, and I will strengthen you. Surrender entirely to Me: every day, every moment. Wait before you rush ahead. Wait for My counsel.

You say it's all about Me. Is it all about Me, or what can I do for you in times of distress? Surrendering means trusting Me, even in times of distress. When you submit totally to Me in every area of your life, you will find such freedom, liberty, and peace: no striving, but the joy of knowing that you are doing My will. For in Me you live and move and have your being. Therefore, prepare your mind for action, be self-controlled, and fully set your hope on the grace given to you when I appear. Continue to trust in My direction. You will bear fruit: fruit that will remain. Fight the good fight of faith, and you will win. Fear will drag you down. Hasn't it done so recently? Trust in Me. Say, "You are my God. My time is in Your hands." It is I, the Lord Jesus Christ, who has called you so that you may show forth the praises of God."

By and by, I settled, and the drive across the three counties continued until the end of the school year. At the start of the summer holiday, I sensed the Holy Spirit encouraging me to start packing. I did, and within two weeks, the kitchen was full of packed brown boxes, awaiting a new home.

Three months later – in November 2011 – we were moving to Harpenden. But leading up to our move, it was a real challenge to keep believing my heart's desire: that we would walk to school. Waiting on God can seem like a slow, painful experience, especially in our need-to-know-now culture. On one occasion, I sat in the car, waiting for school to finish and throwing myself a self-pity party.

"Stop it!"

I had to talk myself out of it. I was in my husband's car and picked up a small devotional book, and read the commentary: 'Jesus' primary consideration is the absolute destruction of my right to myself and my identification with Him. Very few of us truly know what is meant by the absolute "go" of unconditional identification with, abandonment, and surrender to Him.'

After reading that, my self-pity party was certainly over!

When I was driving to ECS, we were the only family traveling from outside Oxfordshire. Most of the families were local to the school.

A HAVEN IN HARPENDEN

At Trinity's new school, I quickly learned that many families drove from surrounding towns, villages, and even from London to Harpenden. A new prayer came into my spirit. Walking to school would be the aim. At ECS, we were a minority. At The King's School, the goal was to keep the same identity. I shared with our daughter and explained that the Bible says, 'Faith without action is dead.' If we were to believe our prayer of walking to school, we would have to do it physically. So, instead of driving up the school drive and parking in the designated area, we began parking the car on the road before the school drive – Bloomfield Road – and walked the rest of the way. People sometimes asked us if we now lived nearby, and I would respond, "Not yet!" On another occasion, I was asked where we hoped to live and replied jokingly, "Around the corner."

Nevertheless, there were times when I doubted, especially as people kept reminding me how expensive Harpenden was, and then proceeded to name neighbouring villages that would be cheaper. One Saturday, we booked several properties to view in the surrounding villages as nothing on my prayer list was coming up in Harpenden: walking distance, a balcony, parking and a garage, central heating and a bath with a shower. However, on the way, I began to feel more and more unwell until the car was stopped, and I threw up. We cancelled all the viewings for the day. Not long after, as I was prayer walking back to school for home time, I sensed,

"Only one thing is mindful here. Not the house prices, not the opinions of others, or any other obstacles that present themselves before you. What are you believing Me for? Only one thing is mindful here, and this is what it is – you want to walk to school – nothing else matters."

I remembered Jesus using those same Words toward Martha: 'Only one thing is mindful.'

"I will find you your desired haven in Harpenden."

But as the weeks passed, and the autumn school term began, we again started to look at properties in the villages around Harpenden. Our tenants would be moving in within weeks, and it seemed time was running out. Early one morning, I went down to our kitchen to pray. My heart was heavy as I laid everything before Lord, and I saw the following in my minds-eye.

I stood alone on the beach looking out across the vast sea stretched before me: it kissed to form the horizon. The sky was a perfect blue and the rays of sunlight were warm on my skin. Behind me were picture-perfect rolling lush, vibrant green hills. Peace permeated the atmosphere. The only sound I could hear was the almost silent waves as they swept across the sand wetting my feet. There was only one question in my mind: why had I been brought here? I became aware of a presence nearby toward my right and turned to look. Our eyes met and we smiled at each other. It was Jesus. I knew I was about to have my question answered.

I felt something roll onto my bare foot. Looking down I saw a pebble, and was instructed to pick it up. I turned and looked to Jesus interpreting His nod without words. It meant I should turn the stone over and read. The word 'Unloved' was written on it and I was instructed to throw it away. Still facing the Lord, I was about to throw it back into the sea and He said,

"No behind you. Throw it into the river behind you."

I turned around and there was a glistening river before me. Its beginning and end were out of view. Light bounced off the surface as though a dance was being performed. A pure shining light that was soft on the eyes. Instantly, I knew which river it was. I was experiencing one of those big, "Wow Lord!" moments. I threw the pebble and it disappeared into the River of Life, the action of which caused a wave of pure love to flood me from within. I turned, and looked at the Lord in sheer delight. Before I had a chance to speak, I was greeted by another pebble rolling onto my foot. Again, I picked it up and this time read the word 'Rejected.' A tinge of sadness started to invade me and I thought to myself, "Quick get rid of it." I threw it into the River of Life and this time the sensation of love was like a fountain bursting through me, felt amazing! Again and again, I picked up pebbles with negative words written on them: 'Unworthy, Pride, Jealousy, Envy, Strife, Bitterness, Greed, Ugly': to name a few. I promptly discarded them into the River of Life. Each time I would be engulfed by a measure of love that radiated from Jesus piercing my whole being: love that had life. I could breathe it in, smell it, hear it and sense it running through my veins. By now I had lost count of how many pebbles I had picked up and discarded. Then the word 'Hatred' appeared, and I looked toward the Lord for an explanation.

"Only by My Spirit can the many works of the flesh be eradicated."

I threw it and my jaw fell open in disbelief when I read the next pebble audibly with a raised voice,

"Murder!"

I turned to the Lord for an explanation but immediately offered mine.

"I wouldn't murder anyone. I've been brought up to be a quiet Catholic girl!"

Another pebble rolled onto my foot and I picked it up. Still waiting for the Lord to respond, my jaw dropped even further as I read, 'Quiet Catholic girl.'

"You are not defined by your upbringing. Nor are you defined by your life experiences or by what people think or say of you. The works of

the flesh may seem very real to you, but they do not define who you are. Neither are you defined by your material wealth or lack of it. Nor how famous you are or how few know of your existence; your intelligence, gifting, or talents. None of the above defines who you are. All things shall pass away and only My Word will remain.

Everything about you is good and wonderful because you were created in My image. I bring healing to broken hearts, complete forgiveness, and acceptance to all. You are defined by My good Spirit. You are defined by the Words printed in My best seller – therein will you find your true self. Your complete identity: spirit, soul and body is in Me"

"Lord, what happens if the pebbles are not thrown into your river?"

"Look behind you."

As I turned round to look, the green rolling hills were no longer there. They were replaced by tall grey jagged mountains. The sky above was grey with heavy dark clouds. As the pebbles with the negative words rolled onto the beach, they would merge at the foot of the mountains causing them to grow and groan. I saw shafts of darkness sweeping across and through them with sharp dagger-like formations appearing. Now and again green hills would seem to appear as if beckoning for freedom and then fade from view into the grey darkness.

"My Spirit is like those green hills yearning for true identity to shine through. See, darkness covers the earth, thick darkness. But I long to rise upon humanity that My glory may be seen.

Look at how you have cried out to me in your distress concerning the journey to school. Look at how you have strived in prayer concerning this matter. Look at how you have repeatedly brought it to My attention, like the persistent widow. Learn from this, as I call you to pray and to intercede. Strive to know the burden of My heart. Strive to know My heartbeat. The anguish I feel for a dying world. Then, you will understand what it means to be a watchman in the tower. Seeing – with advanced understanding."

I was happy to stay on that beach all day but I noticed the time was 7am. I had to pull myself away and get our daughter up for school. It was a short supernatural visit to the beach that morning, but an unforgettable one.

The following day I had an appointment to see our daughter's teacher. I climbed the stairs and as I opened the door my heart welcomed what I saw on the display board created by the children – a glistening river bearing the title River of Life.

Three days later, I walked out to the playground on playtime duty, and there in the sky was a brightly coloured rainbow over the school.

A HAVEN IN HARPENDEN

"I keep my promises. Your haven is coming."

They were glad when it grew calm, and he guided them to their desired haven.
Psalm 107:30

Two days later, when driving home from school, all I kept hearing in my spirit was, "I just want to walk to school." I started to speak it out aloud again and again, to the point of annoyance in my daughter's ears,

"Mum, why do you keep saying that? You sound like a parrot!"

Back home in the kitchen, I sensed the Holy Spirit urging me to contact an estate agent to ask them if a flat advertised had a garage. I was sure it didn't have a garage because I had already contacted them previously, so I was puzzled why I was given this instruction. After constant nudging, I eventually called them. The rental agent explained that she was usually in another branch and would have to check the details. Sure enough, there was no garage. Then she explained that someone had just popped in with new property details about a flat. She kept me on hold again and, on returning, explained,

"It's a two-bedroom apartment with a garage on Bloomfield Road in Harpenden. Do you know where it is?"

"Do I know where it is?" I thought, "It's the first road around the corner from The King's School that our daughter attends. The very road where we parked the car and walked!"

Could this be the fulfilment of God's promise? The following day, George, Trinity, and I viewed the vacant flat after school, and in my spirit, I knew it was our *"haven."* Everything on our list received a tick. The most significant tick was that we would walk to school. Three days later, I had the key in my hand. It was real. I had the key in my hand.

The first day we walked up the hill to school felt terrific and Trinity asked,

"Mum, do you know when we were believing in God that we would walk to school?"

"Yes," I responded.

"That was hard!"

"Yes, it was. But we did it."

ONE LICK!

For the wages of sin is death, but the free gift of God is eternal life in Christ Jesus.

Romans 6:23

I believe there is a longing discernment, that only a relationship with the living God can fill in the deepest psyche of who we are as human beings. I haven't always been a Christian. No one is born one, even if they are brought up in a Christian family. I was brought up in the Catholic branch of Christianity, but I didn't know Jesus personally. He was an image on the inside of church buildings and appeared in stories told at catechism. Now that I have been a follower of Jesus for almost 40 years, the manuscript of my life in Him is a reflection, a reality of His presence here on earth.

On the day I became a Christian – 7th July 1985 – the sun was blazing, and the sky was a perfect blue. I was sitting in a friend's car with an ice cream in my hand. The night before, I had presented a challenge to God. After months of searching and questioning, I concluded that I would trust myself to make a firm decision. The impact would be immediate, and my life's journey ahead unknown. But I was prepared to wait and see how things would unfold. I spoke out my ultimatum.

"I understand that I'm a sinner, and Your death releases me from that if I repent and accept You into my life. But I'm not interested in You (God) unless You speak to me. Unless You show yourself to be real in my everyday life, how will I know how real You are? Otherwise, You'll be just like any other god! I've read books about You where You speak to Christians. I know that I'm not anyone special in church, and You know that I don't even go to church regularly, so why would You talk to me? But if You don't speak to me, how will I know You really exist? How will I know that You're any different from all the other gods that I teach? I've not yet met a Buddhist, a Hindu, or a Muslim who says their god speaks to them. I've even spoken to Christians who say that God doesn't speak to them. But I'm convinced that You do speak. I've read about it and have heard others share about it. I want to hear You speaking to me as You do to others. Would that be possible?"

I licked my ice cream numerous times, trying to interrupt the flow of it melting further down the cone, and my friend asked me a question,

ONE LICK!

"Are you ready to give your life to Jesus?"

My own words from the previous day were still fresh in my mind. Would He talk to me? Would He even notice me and my little life tucked away in the corner of this big wide world? Am I about to do something that would drastically change my life? Should I say "Yes" or "No?"

"Why all these questions?" I asked myself. Why was I hesitant? I had already made up my mind the night before. I took another lick of my ice cream and responded,

"Yes, I'm ready."

Are you?

Printed in Great Britain
by Amazon